Gianmaria Buccellati
Art in Gold, Silver and Gems

Smithsonian
National Museum of Natural History

BUCCELLATI
Art in Gold, Silver and Gems

Edited by Maria Cristina Buccellati

Art Director
Marcello Francone

Editorial Coordination
Marzia Branca

Editing
Emanuela Di Lallo

Layout
Monica Temporiti

Translations from Italian
Lawrence Jenkens

Photographs
Renato Zuccolin
Giuliano Plorutti (cover)

*The texts on Mario Buccellati and the history
of jewelry are by Gianni Roggini;
the interview to Gianmaria Buccellati
and the entries of the chapter "Precious Objects"
are by Benedetta Barzini*

First published in Italy in 2000
by Skira Editore S.p.A.
Palazzo Casati Stampa
via Torino 61, 20123 Milano (Italy)

Printed and bound in Italy. First edition

Distributed in North America and Latin America
by Abbeville Publishing Group, 22 Cortlandt Street,
New York, NY 10007, USA.
Distributed elsewhere in the world by Thames and
Hudson Ltd., 181a High Holborn, London WC1V
7QX, United Kingdom.

It is especially meaningful to introduce an exhibit like that organized by the Smithsonian Institution here in Washington in honor of Gianmaria Buccellati.

In fact, it takes on unique significance because the works on exhibit reflect the remarkable creativity of a great goldsmith, Buccellati, over the span of so many years. This, in combination with his extraordinary, even inimitable, ability to maintain such a strong success with the public. In short, I see Buccellati's work as a perfect synthesis of creativity and design. It also reflects — and I would be remiss, in my capacity as Ambassador of Italy to the United States, not to mention this — thoroughly Italian qualities, which have always been widely recognized.

Together with sculpture and engraving, jewelry and silverwork have for centuries been a specialty of Italian artists. Coming to mind in this context is the story of one of the master goldsmiths and sculptors of the Renaissance, who had a presentiment of his calling to this noble profession early in youth. In his autobiography Cellini vividly recalls a childhood vision of a salamander frolicking in the flames of the hearth, foreshadowing the destiny that awaited him. It is ever so intriguing that many years later Mark Twain makes reference to that same image.

But no matter how or when Buccellati came to recognize his talent, of one thing I am certain, his creations have already left their impression; the evidence is this marvelous exhibit. And with this, I invite the readers of this catalog and the visitors to the exhibit here in Washington to "explore" these works as if taking a precious excursion through artistic expression.

Ferdinando Salleo
Ambassador of Italy to the United States

Contents

My family's goldsmith roots go back to about the mid-eighteenth century when our ancestor, Contardo Buccellati, had his own shop in Via degli Orafi (today's Via Orefici) in Milan. He was considered at the time to be the most important goldsmith in the Lombardy region. Then the name faded in the Milanese fog…

It was soon after the First World War that my father, Mario Buccellati, established a shop carrying his own name that was located at Via Santa Margherita, near the famous La Scala theater. It was here that he launched what has become known as the famous "Buccellati Style".

From the very beginning, his shop was frequented by poets, writers, musicians, composers, prominent artists, and patrons. The famous Italian poet, Gabriele D'Annunzio, dubbed him "Prince of Goldsmiths", heir to the renown Italian tradition begun during the Renaissance by Benvenuto Cellini, one of the greatest artists of all times. Like his famous ancestor, my father designed and executed his jewels in a sort of "complicity" with his clients. His jewels were unique pieces that were skillfully and carefully handcrafted… simply perfect.

I drew my first design at the age of twelve. My father thought that I had a natural talent for designing and creativity and allowed me to "grow up" imbued with the art, culture, and beauty that filled his shop. I, therefore, treasure the peculiar style of the Buccellati House, begun as far back as the eighteenth century.

While my father concentrated mainly on jewels, I have found equal satisfaction in designing jewels, as well as silver.

I inherited from my father his art and craft, the technical secrets, and the aesthetic canons, which I now transmit to my own children. We have created a modern blending of trends and taste, leading to the execution of pieces that are always faithful to our family tradition.

The jewels, one-of-a-kind silver pieces, and the special "museum pieces" which are presented here, are a retrospective of many of the most important ones executed by my father and myself. This constitutes the basis of the legacy that will be transferred to the entire Buccellati family.

I dedicate this exhibition to my father who started it all; and to my family that will carry on this tradition. I present this collection with great pride and satisfaction, and hope that it will be a true source of enjoyment for you.

Gianmaria Buccellati
Milan, September 2000

Introduction

The History of Pre-eminence of the Italian Goldsmiths' Art

Jewelry with the label "made in Italy" is recognized around the world for its extraordinary quality, its superior harmony and its irresistible appeal. The extraordinary technical ability of Italian goldsmiths lies at the source of this recognized supremacy, but more important is their capacity to rework and synthesize the broad range of their cultural patrimony.

Traces of the great cultures of the past are today part of the Italian goldsmiths' genetic makeup. This heritage, from the Egyptians to ancient Mesopotamia, from the Aegean civilizations to the Greek world, from the Etruscans to the Romans, from Byzantium to the Barbarians, is constantly being rediscovered and reinterpreted in original ways. From this point of view the sometimes unhappy history of Italy has created a unique layering of cultures which is at the heart of the "popular good taste" which marks the peninsula.

Great schools of jewelers flourished as early as the Middle Ages. In Siena, for example, the technique of translucent enamel work was perfected in the second half of the thirteenth century and was then adopted by craftsmen of the Meuse and Rhine valley schools, as well as in Paris. Pace di Valentino and then Guccio di Mannaia produced extraordinary works using this technique which is based on the transparency of enamel that allows the figures underneath it, engraved with varying degrees of forcefulness on a metal surface — usually silver — a strong sense of chiaroscuro modeling. Vasari wrote about it "as a kind of painting combined with sculpture". Benvenuto Cellini said that "enamel work is nothing else but painting".

In 1338 the Sienese craftsman Ugolino di Vieri made what is considered the masterpiece of medieval Italian goldsmiths' work, the monumental reliquary of the Corporal in the Cathedral of Orvieto. The great painter Simone Martini had already tried, in his *Maestà* in Siena for example, to reproduce the preciousness of enamel using a technique of etched, gilded glass that was known in antiquity but then abandoned by the Byzantines. At the end of the fourteenth century Cennino Cennini accurately described this process in his *Libro dell'arte* noting that it involved applying a very thin layer of gold to the back of glass with egg white and then etching it — a technique which allowed for no errors.

Without a doubt, however, the Renaissance was the time of greatest success for Italian jewelers for in this period Italy reigned supreme throughout Europe for the design and decoration of jewelry. And yet it was precisely in this historical and cultural context that the distinction — destined to remain in place for centuries — between the major arts (painting, sculpture and architecture) and the minor arts was first made. While painters, sculptors and architects were recognized as cultured figures, that is intellectuals, the other crafts were relegated to the less noble sphere of the artisan.

Goldsmiths, too, because they were involved in an activity that was essentially decorative, one in which ornamental motifs predominated, were grouped with craftsmen rather than artists. This was a step backwards in comparison to their status in the mid-thirteenth century when Etienne Boileau, in his *Livre des métiers*, defined goldsmithing as "the art of kings" and put it at the top of his list of the arts and professions of his time.

It is also true, however, that goldsmiths always enjoyed good social standing because they were highly appreciated as makers of luxury goods, as the designers and creators of objects which were valuable both for their material and for the workmanship involved in making them. (Aldous Huxley wrote that every jewel is the sum of two magic elements, the material and human invention.) The nature of their work itself allows goldsmiths to maintain, at least to a certain degree, the ancient dignity of *luxuriae ministri* and to stay in contact with the most distinguished members of today's society. Their aesthetic sense, for example, is universally appreciated. In 1504, for instance, in Florence a committee of thirty experts was appointed to find a suitable place for Michelangelo's *David*: of them six were goldsmiths or jewelers and one was a famous carver of gemstones.

It is interesting to note, too, the importance assigned to the art of the goldsmith in an artist's training: the apprentice goldsmith in the typical Renaissance workshop followed a rigorous course of study. This was true for Brunelleschi and Ghiberti, for Michelozzo and Pollaiolo, and for Paolo Uccello, Andrea del Sarto, Verrocchio and Ghirlandaio. Verrocchio and Ghirlandaio later trained Leonardo da Vinci and Michelangelo respectively as apprentices in their own shops.

Splendid objects were produced during the Renaissance using the ancient technique of *niello*. It was known in the Graeco-Roman period, was widely used by Byzantine craftsmen and then in the Arab world, and was finally "rediscovered" by Italian, and more precisely Tuscan, goldsmiths. This method consists of filling lines engraved into gold or silver with a dark alloy (*nigellum*) made of red copper, silver, saffron-colored sulphur and lead with a little bit of borax added. The results are captivating.

One of the most unusual artists of all times, Benvenuto Cellini, defined himself as a goldsmith his entire life and never hid his preference for craft or his pride in his own manual ability. Indeed, it was these qualities which gave him the right to move as an equal amongst painters and sculptors. The proof of this comes, from among other things, in the fact that he wrote treatises which dealt with technical rather than theoretical issues. As Maria Grazia Ciardi Duprè has pointed out, "Cellini, as a goldsmith by trade, was aware of the independent formal and expressive value of pure ornament". It was exactly his experience as a goldsmith which he brought to his monumental sculpture. A good example of this, ignoring the very famous salt-cellar he designed for Cardinal Ippolito d'Este and then executed for Francis I of France, is the highly decorated base of the *Perseus*, a superb instance of the virtuosity of the goldsmith.

Not many years after Cellini died, however, the situation changed radically and largely because of another Italian "phenomenon", that is the birth of the academies. One finds, for example, that Stefano Della Bella, an important engraver and scenery designer at the French courts under Richelieu and Mazarin, had his apprenticeship as a goldsmith abruptly ended because it seemed "awkward to keep a young man so skilled in design in a craft where good design is very necessary but in a fairly limited and narrow field which extends, at the most, to making a few things well, while in painting all the works of nature itself are objects to be imitated".

Excluded from the important cultural currents, goldsmiths became enslaved by the whims of fashion. They lost, definitively, any claim to the stature of artists and were relegated, instead, to the category of technicians. It is significant that one of the first Italian institutions for scientific research — the Accademia del Cimento, founded in Florence in 1657 — took its name from a technical term used in goldsmithing: *cimento* means, in fact, testing the degree of purity in gold.

Even after the Renaissance, from the Baroque and Rococo periods to the era of revivals and Art Nouveau, there have been excellent goldsmiths and jewelers. Yet it was not until Mario Buccellati came along that the image, even in Italy, of the great goldsmith capable of creating his own easily recognizable style (thus freeing him from the constraints of fashion trends) re-emerged. Indeed he was able to reclaim the full status of an artist amongst the cultural elite of his own time.

The Buccellati Style:
The Creation of Beauty

The works of art produced by three generations of the Buccellati family can be compared to the Renaissance tradition of craftsmanship innate in the workshops of Venice, Florence, Rome and Milan. In truth every city in medieval Europe had many families of artisans, and it was the accumulation of their knowledge and experience that gave rise to exceptional artists like Benvenuto Cellini, the enamel masters of Limoges or the tapestry weavers at Goblins.

The history of the Buccellati family is especially interesting because both Gianmaria and his son, Andrea, have continued to work in the tradition of the company's founder and Gianmaria's father, Mario. The combination of idea or concept, design and the specialized craftsmen who execute the pieces, capable of exploring as they create, is a perfect one. Furthermore, of Mario's many children, only Gianmaria had a designer's temperament, and of his three children, Andrea was the only one to inherit his father's creative ability.

There are some things in this world which will never change, even with more advanced technologies and the evolution of new economies. These things exist on a plane above ideologies, where "modernity" is something permanent and where beauty exists, first and foremost, in the mystery of the process of shaping an object from a drawing and only afterwards in the aesthetics of the work. Beauty can be interpreted in many ways, but beyond the vagaries of changing fashions, beauty has but one form which is universally recognized by the human soul.

The Buccellati family has had a dialogue with beauty since the eighteenth century, although it has only officially been in the business of creating objects for three generations. For them, the beauty of precious metals and stones has always worked to serve the finished piece. Beauty is the challenge between the idea of it, human hands and the possibility of realizing it. An object signed by Mario, Gianmaria or Andrea Buccellati radiates the inestimable value of past eras which gave form to it and the extraordinary play of solids and voids and of gemstones and metal which give the viewer a sense of pure magic.

Every inch of each piece has been carefully worked. The time spent is absolutely necessary to make the separate elements of the work — the chasing or the set stones — come to life as the craftsman creates the individual piece.

Important human creations are never made in a hurry, and thus the value of quality does not change over the centuries. It is not by chance that the temples of ancient times majestically dominate, in the silence of centuries, the underlying chaos that originally surrounded them. Gianmaria Buccellati might spend twenty years finishing one object knowing that with the next the struggle over every detail will arise again. He knows that poetry clashes with the material and that the challenge rolls, wave after wave, from problem to solution and towards workmanship that is ever more intricate and results that are always more delicate. Complexity disappears in the lightness of the jewelry and assumes harmonious gravity in pieces such as the rock crystal amphora, or the cups and the boxes.

My father did not teach me working techniques just as I did not teach them to my son. What happened was the transmission of an idea, a vision, the experience of working and the assimilation of tradition. I wanted to "steal" my father's ideas, and I think that my son, Andrea, wants to rob me of mine in order to add them to his and to define an identity different from mine or that of his grandfather, just as my hand is different from my father's...

We have each, after absorbing the fundamental principles of our history, acted according to our own instincts. When we create the metal structure of an object to set the stones, for example, we still use hand tools because an electric drill produces inferior results.

Two ingredients are necessary to achieve the quality of work required by the Buccellati spirit. They are an expression of individual personality that influences both the design and the execution of the object, and the availability and patience of passionate craftsmanship. The sons and grandsons of Mario Buccellati's original craftsmen still work at Buccellati today, and they have been joined by a new generation of artisans prepared to follow in the historical footsteps of the founder.

Mario Buccellati's brilliance came in capturing the spirit of the craft of goldsmithing through old but time-tested techniques in order to achieve original results.

He was a man with a powerful, violent and impatient spirit. He had a very strong personality. He worked intuitively, and his designs alluded to an idea which his craftsmen had to know how to interpret.

At the age of fifteen Gianmaria was working alongside his father, and at that time he was afraid that he would never be Mario's equal and worried that he could not earn the respect of the workers. In contrast to his father's working style, though, he became a patient, meticulous designer whose drawings were immediately comprehensible. Mario Buccellati believed that there was nothing to be learned from the jeweler-goldsmith, and this forced Gianmaria to lie to him: in order to learn he used to tell his father that he was going to the movies with friends, and instead he would go to the craftsmen's shops to watch them work or to a classmate's house to study the history of art...

My son Andrea has an even more difficult life. He found techniques that have been perfected and workshops that are finely tuned, and even more important, he has a father who is still very active. The real problem is that the number of objects created is much larger than what I inherited at his age. Furthermore, the value of the name "Buccellati" has grown. Andrea is more meticulous, precise and geometric than I am. He has the tenacity of his forefathers, and like them, he does his work with a sense of humility. It is hard to explain, but we care about the effort and the energy which we devote to making piece after piece; each object is for us a source of pleasure.

The objects we make are born in our imagination and in the contemplation of art, but the source of each creation can be found in memory, reminiscences and dreams...

And jewelry, if it does not decorate a woman's face, is neither interesting or lovely.

The woman must always outshine the object she wears.

Gianmaria Buccellati's favorite necklaces are those that reflect the gracefulness of the big Venetian lace collars of the seventeenth century.

Those people truly captivated by Buccellati are the few who love memory, culture and knowledge. They prefer the most hidden qualities of a piece which are increased by the effort spent in making it and the time required to engrave into stone the hope of perfection.

My father also worked for the Vatican, and the Belgian and English courts; he worked for the nobility and had a special relationship with the writer Gabriele D'Annunzio. I work for the person who values this search for..., for a sufficient number of people. They know how to appreciate a unique and rare object.

I am content to know that my work can be found all over the world and that it is far away from me. This allows room in my mind for new ideas. If, however, I see something my father or I designed in an antique shop or for sale at auction, I buy it willingly. I remember how we made it and how we resolved the problems it posed. They are like an old friend found again...

It is impossible to imitate the creations of Mario, Gianmaria or Andrea Buccellati. At least six craftsmen oversee each piece at every phase of its creation. When there are breaks in this process, Buccellati checks on the progress being made and the proportions of the piece. Sometimes months or even years go by between each stage in the creation of an object, and sometimes Buccellati chooses to start over again with a new design and work then begins from scratch. It is possible to copy a style, but to copy a creation of Buccellati is truly impossible.

Beauty is less an aesthetic fact than a mystical idea. I do not, for example, worry about the value of the stones as I work. What counts for me is the preciousness of the work as a whole, its uniqueness, without having to justify it.

An object by Buccellati does not flaunt its beauty but rather offers it. To possess something by Buccellati is like owning a historical treasure, a testament of respect and love for human skill, for the mythological tradition, for the traces history has left on the wrinkles of time. This trace is even more meaningful because today the word "unique" is rare, and the memory of the one who uses new technologies without having learned the beauty of heartfelt passion becomes really tenuous.

Mario Buccellati: Prince of Goldsmiths

Mario Buccellati was born in 1891 in Ancona, although all of his family came from the Lombardy region, in the north of Italy. He had ancestral precedents for the career he chose in producing precious objects. In the mid-eighteenth century the goldsmith Contardo Buccellati was active in Milan where he had a workshop on Via degli Orafi (today Via Orefici), very close to the city's Cathedral.

Mario's father died when his son was very young; his mother moved first to Lomellina and then to Milan, where he was apprenticed to the famous goldsmiths' firm Beltrami & Besnati. In 1919, after the First World War had come to an end, the former apprentice took over the business. He gave it his name and embarked on an adventure which would bring him international fame.

Mario Buccellati's jewelry fascinates because it is classic and at the same time new. References to the great pieces of the Renaissance are clear in his work, yet his ability to interpret these models from the past in a very personal way is also obvious. Every object he made has a special, unique and easily identifiable quality which came quickly to be known as the "Buccellati style" and a legend in contemporary jewelry making. The Buccellati style has survived through the decades by continuously redefining itself.

Mario's jewelry, which demonstrated his absolute mastery of combining the goldsmith's art and an unfathomable sense of fantasy, very quickly attracted an important clientele. Members of the royal houses of Italy, Spain and Egypt fell in love with them, popes and cardinals appreciated them and cultured people everywhere praised them. Like Contardo's workshop, Mario Buccellati's store was very close to the Milanese Cathedral and nearby two of the other important symbols of that city, the theater of La Scala and the Galleria. This store quickly became a meeting place for refined and exacting clients, as well as intellectuals.

The famous poet Gabriele D'Annunzio was among the latter group. He dubbed Mario the "Prince of Goldsmiths" and later, with more imagination, "Mastro Paragon Coppella" which translates, roughly, to the "Exemplary Master of the Crucible". The initial friendship between the author and the goldsmith soon became a true comradeship based on a spiritual understanding, a sense of complicity and mutual admiration. There are copious records of this relationship, and it even survived D'Annunzio's chronic and rather human faults.

Over a seventeen-year period, the Italian romantic poet commissioned literally hundreds of gifts all made especially for him by Buccellati. He gave to everybody, everywhere. D'Annunzio was a generous man: diamond bracelets were as casual to him as greeting cards. He would "dedicate" a jewel box to a beautiful Lady, accompanied by a few poetic words and then send it to his great friend to be filled.

One occasion, when D'Annunzio was paying court to Ida Rubinstein of the Paris Opera, he dispatched two such boxes to the jeweler. They were duly filled with diamond treasures and returned to the poet. Before he could bestow them on Madame Rubinstein, however — she was touring with her Company — another charmer came along. So Gabriele D'Annunzio unselfishly emptied the caskets for her benefit and returned them urgently to his friend to be filled again. D'Annunzio remembered exactly what each piece looked like and in his letter of command to the jeweler he speaks of the glowing "arabesque of diamonds" weaving in and around some darker stones.

Gabriele D'Annunzio, had a long romance also with Eleonora Duse, the greatest actress of her time, who encouraged him to write theater pieces. D'Annunzio, in fact, dedicated many of his masterworks to her.

Among the numerous pieces that Buccellati created for Gabriele D'Annunzio, the most interesting are the "Teca dei Lupi di Toscana", now in the Museum at the Vittoriale, and his personal "heroic cigarette cases", in which the Commander's glorious undertakings are inscribed.

He wrote so many letters to his friend Mario, all of them on hand-made paper and all of them hand-written. "My Dear

Buccellati you know all too well that I, poor sinner that I am, can never resist temptation!", the poet would write, in one dated December 11, 1922. In another the poet dubbed again Mario Buccellati, calling him "Mastro Paragon Coppella" and "Master of the Precious Metal", stating that this would be the name by which Mario would thereafter be known among men. When a letter was finished, D'Annunzio would fold and tie it with yards of red and blue ribbon, the colors of his princely house and send it all the way to Milan from Lake Garda (some sixty miles away) by courier. And of course he expected a reply by the same messenger…

In the wake of his success, Mario Buccellati opened a second store in Rome, on Via Condotti, in 1925, and in 1929 his now famous sign was also prominent in Florence, on Via Tornabuoni and in the vicinity of Palazzo Strozzi, one of the masterpieces of Renaissance architecture. Mario was also interested in expanding abroad, although it would be more than twenty years before he was able to do so. In 1951, after the Second World War, Mario's oldest son, Luca, opened a small store on 51st Street in New York. The store then moved, only a few years later, to much larger quarters on the city's famous Fifth Avenue.

Luca was the first of Mario Buccellati's five sons, all but one of whom became involved in their father's business. Lorenzo took charge of the company's administration and coordinated its various areas, Federico ran the stores in Rome and Florence, and Gianmaria ran the store in Milan and also assisted his father in designing and producing objects. Only Giorgio, the youngest, was more attracted by the academic world: he became a noticed scholar of archaeology, philology and linguistics. Mario's four older sons inherited their father's business in 1965, when, at the age of 74, he died after reigning for decades as "the" Italian jeweler. In 1967 the company's headquarters in Milan moved from Via Santa Margherita to Via Montenapoleone, and two years later the brothers separated their interests. Lorenzo and Federico chose to run the three stores in Italy, and Luca and Gianmaria took charge of the company in the United States. Gianmaria also took over the production of jewelry and silverware, determined to consolidate and expand the achievement of the "Buccellati style" in the most important countries in the world.

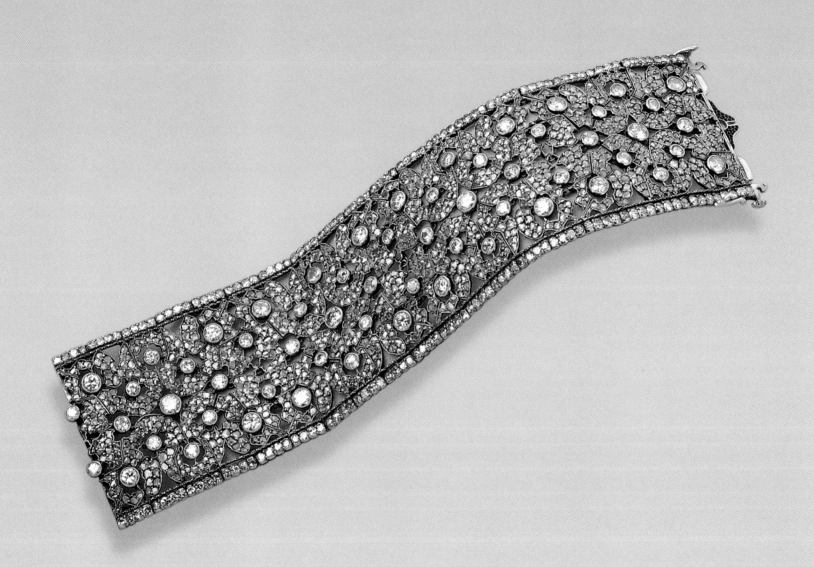

GIAN MARIA
BUCCELLATI
RICORDO DELLA
SUA PRIMA
S. COMUNIONE
18 APRILE 1957

E S. CRESIMA
11 MAGGIO 1957
NELLA CAPPEL-
LA DELL'ISTITU
TO GONZAGA
IN MILANO

ACCEDITE AD CHRISTUM ET SATIAMINI
QUIA PANIS EST; POTATE QUIA FONS EST;
ILLUMINAMINI QUIA LUX EST.

Gianmaria Buccellati:
The Evolution of a Designer

The world of 1969 was one of rapid cultural change. Travel by airplane was becoming more common… The expression "jet set" was first coined during this period to describe high-profile individuals who crisscrossed the globe for business and for pleasure. Gianmaria Buccellati recognized that the world was becoming a smaller place. If Mario Buccellati was, indeed, ahead of his time when he opened shops in New York and in Palm Beach in the years after the Second World War, it was Gianmaria who realized his father's dream of building a truly international recognition for the family name.

It was in this time of 1969 that Gianmaria, who retained his father's manufactory and now on his own after separating his interests from his three older brothers, embarked on his journey. He always maintained a close alliance with Luca, his beloved older brother, who moved to New York in 1951. Together, the brothers built on the strong foundation set by their father. Along with jewels, the silver, especially, with the introduction of a rich treasury of sterling flatware, established the company among the most influential circles. The spacious and luxurious salon on the famous Fifth Avenue set a high standard for a glamorous and high-profile clientele that shopped there.

Gianmaria recognized that Asia was a region with a tradition of artistic elegance and appreciation for the kind of jewels and silver sculpture for which his firm excelled. In rapid succession, Gianmaria established selling relationships in Hong Kong, in 1970; and in Japan, in 1972. He also began to court the wealthy Americans and Europeans who flocked to Italy in the 1970s and 1980s and established himself in the resorts of Sardinia, Capri, and Elba Island; and in Milan and Venice in the 1980s. In addition, he opened a shop in Monte Carlo in 1976.

However, it is with the opening of a glamorous salon in Paris' prestigious Place Vendôme in 1979, that he established himself as a jeweler of world-class renown. The elegant square in Paris is home to the world's main jewelers; Gianmaria was the first important Italian to have a shop there, just as Mario was the first to have one on Fifth Avenue in New York. The opening of a beautiful salon in the Regent Beverly Wilshire Hotel in Beverly Hills in 1989 completed the coast-to-coast expansion in the United States.

Today, Gianmaria at seventy-one years still works vigorously alongside family members, including his wife, Rosa Maria Bresciani, who is active in the commercial sector. The third generation of Buccellati family members is equally active. Gino, his eldest son, manages silver production outside of Bologna; Andrea, the inheritor of his father's and grandfather's creative legacy, works at his side for the design and production of jewelry; and Maria Cristina, his only daughter, creates the advertising and publicity for the Milan-based firm. Mario, II, his nephew (the son of his brother, Luca) manages the New York operation, as did his father before him.

The jewels designed by Gianmaria Buccellati in the latter half of the twentieth century vividly illustrate the master's respect for the Renaissance-period techniques perfected by his father, with the particular aesthetic that was equally influenced by the French Rococo period. Gianmaria's jewelry designs reflect a more adventurous spirit, which aptly represents the times of his ascendancy. It is interesting to study the evolution of his style, one that was more influenced by his father's stricter aesthetic in the period after Mario's death; to a wildly imaginative phase that began in the late 1970s and 1980s, a period when he enjoyed particular success personally, artistically, and commercially. That evolution continues today as he prepares Andrea for his own ascendancy.

The jewels exhibited reflect the designer's strong personality and keen eye. While other famous houses have focused their attention on large gemstones, such as diamonds, rubies, emeralds and sapphires in simple settings, Gianmaria Buccellati has pursued design that focuses on unique settings for unique stones. His jewels illustrate the designer's love of unusual pearls, precious and semi-precious gemstones, minerals, even "rough diamonds", which are combined in ways to create one-of-a-kind pieces of great drama without the usual "heaviness" associated with objects of great importance. It is said that Gianmaria's jewels "move" with their wearer due to their great flexibility and ingenious design.

The designer has assembled a rich collection of his extraordinary jeweled pieces for this exhibition by borrowing a number of items from his family, his most faithful clients and friends. The exhibition traces the evolution of his style and highlights only a fraction of an impressive body of work created over a lifetime. Equally impressive are the "Precious Objects", many combining the techniques of the master jeweler with the master silversmith, starting with those designed by Mario Buccellati in the 1920s.

Among the marvels on display are sixteen "masterworks": one-of-a-kind chalices, candlesticks, coffers, and other forms created with precious metals, and gemstones. Designed by Gianmaria since 1970, these objects attest to the continuation of a superb level of craftsmanship in contemporary Italy. The making of the works involved extremely difficult manual techniques, some of them rarely practiced today. Of particular note are finely engraved surfaces, a Buccellati hallmark. The works offer inventive re-interpretation of various aesthetic conventions from the past, particularly those of ancient Rome, the Italian Renaissance, and eighteenth-century France. These sixteen works have been created over the last thirty years and will remain in the family's private collection as their "legacy".

One piece that is already pre-destined is the cup that has been named "Smithsonian Cup". This piece has been completed in 2000 to coincide with the opening of the exhibition at the Smithsonian Institution. It took nearly 24 years of on again-off again work… as Gianmaria searched for the best solution to the enhancement of a carved cup of gray Brazilian agate. Decorated with white and yellow gold and silver and embellished with pearls, the cup is a splendid example of craftsmanship that is nearly impossible today.

As he marks his sixth decade of work, Gianmaria isn't quite finished yet! He continues to challenge himself and his beloved artisans in an effort to scale new artistic and aesthetic heights.

Gianmaria Buccellati: "Precious Objects"

The Making of the Smithsonian Cup

A cup is an evocative object. It is the chalice of pleasure and contains the exaltation of life, its elixir, the exquisite nectar of the gods. It suggests meetings and invites hope. It unites physical and intellectual satisfaction and spirituality with materiality.

I have always designed cups. Not necessarily to sell, but to experience a dialogue with a stone that I found somewhere. Every stone has a mystery… a story waiting to be told. This gray agate (variegated chalcedony) inspired me to look for a harmony between something full and something empty in an attempt to give the object a sort of "re-birth", which I always want in art.

Working a cup allows me to think about the dilemma and the challenge of how to appropriately cover a stone with decorations. The cup that I have dedicated to the Smithsonian existed in my mind or on the goldsmith's worktables for twenty-four years! Although it was not a continuous process, this is the time that I needed to resolve the challenges that the agate posed for me.

It was cut with notches at irregular intervals on the upper edge. At first, I wanted a design that was based on a conch shell, but the stone's dimensions were not the right proportions. My second idea was to enlarge the edge of the agate with a silver border in order to attach a trim or "fesonatura" to hide the notches. As it was being assembled, however, I was not satisfied with this solution. The border disturbed the harmony of the whole.

For a long time I drew new ideas for the border, but none of them worked. Years passed before I found the answer in simplifying the mount with a central decorative motif made with mounted stones and a three-tiered border. Even this solution, though, was not right, and more time passed before the idea of ruches with "fesonated" bases came to me. Finally, I was able to get the right proportions between the base and the top of the cup.

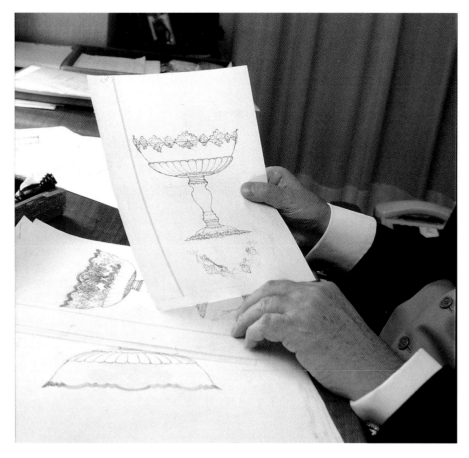

The "fesoni" are not symmetrical because of the notches in the stone, but I compensated for this by balancing it with a frieze with an uneven border in order to match the curves of the "fesonatura".

The above phases in just designing the piece lasted twenty years, and the remaining four were spent actually making the cup. Although it stretched the patience of the craftsmen (and even mine, sometimes), much time was also spent evaluating and thinking about the results at each stage. The truly special quality of the cup, however, is found in the dynamic of the elements — fastenings and pins — which hold the work together.

Every cup brings something festive with it, the idea of joy rather than that of victory or a prize. The cup is a symbol of conviviality. The conviviality of the Smithsonian Cup in particular, is reminiscent of the Baroque period and the eighteenth century in France, where gold and silver and precious stones were mixed with the architecture of design.

This particular cup is "dedicated" to the Smithsonian Institution because the offer to have this exhibition came at the time when we had hit on the final concept for the piece. Designing cups for me has a sentimental value. It is a type of creativity, which I have in my soul. The Smithsonian Cup was the most difficult project because I wanted to harmonize its irregularities. It was not so much a sense of symmetry that worried me as one of harmony, the indispensable element in defining the form of beauty.

Gianmaria Buccellati

CUP OF PLEASURE

1975

In the past, the chalice served liturgical purposes and stood as a prized possession in the private cabinets of European aristocracy, symbolizing the wealth and power of its owner. In the style of the best Italian Renaissance and French Rococo taste, the Cup of Pleasure represents the essence of Buccellati craftsmanship.

This chalice, created from three pieces of carved rock crystal (colorless quartz) is joined together with yellow, white and pink gold and embellished by rubies and emeralds.

Private collection Gianmaria Buccellati

CUP OF THE SPIRIT OF LOVE

1974

Created in a Rococo motif, the cup is a hymn to the elegance of feminine forms inspiring the highest image of the spirit of love. Decorated around an ancient piece of red jasper, the motifs are known as "ruches". Realized in extreme relief, Venus and three Cupids move as if in water, air or wind.

The sculptures show how goldsmithing can reach the summit of artistic inspiration close to other sorts of figurative arts. Base and stem are bordered and decorated with yellow gold chased in torsadé motifs, using the lost wax technique.

Private collection Gianmaria Buccellati

CUP OF EUPHORIC BLISS

1978

The style is inspired by the beauty of swans as seen in art since the Greek Hellenistic period. Gianmaria Buccellati was inspired to create a swan by the shape of the piece of moss jasper.

The swan "melts" itself around the cup. Its gold chest and wings embrace the stone while neck and head sinuously look upon the body. The base incorporates two gold and silver rings, leaf motif set with faceted emeralds.

Private collection Gianmaria Buccellati

CUP OF MUSES

1981

With Neoclassical proportions and shape, this trophy takes its inspiration from Graeco-Roman traditions. Carved into an exceptional piece of pure jade, the myth of the Nine Muses evokes an emotional creativity enhanced by the precious and dramatic contrast of its colors.

Made of gold and silver, the trophy is encrusted with 2027 cabochon sapphires. Inside the gold border are finely engraved the names of the Nine Muses.

Private collection Gianmaria Buccellati

ROCK-CRYSTAL CANDLESTICKS

1971

The design of these candlesticks symbolically recalls the passion for elaborate beauty that reigned at the court of Louis XIV, in his newly built palace of Versailles.

Created of pure natural crystal, they are embellished with silver that is worked with engraving and shading techniques. The candlesticks are an example of creative and technical capacities that are still vigorously alive in the present time.

Private collection Gianmaria Buccellati

Triumphal Amphora

1996

Echoing the marvels of the Renaissance, the rock-crystal amphora is enhanced by embossed foliage decorations pinpointed with gold motifs and cabochon sapphires. Internally carved and externally festooned, the amphora bears two stylized crests in the center.

The pattern of stylized leaves is executed in yellow gold and enhances two cabochon lapis lazuli from Afghanistan.

A rock-crystal base supports festoon-carved motifs linked to the amphora with opposing silver stylized leaves and a series of matching scroll decorations, similar to those around the top opening. The sculptured handles flow from the body of the amphora and are enriched by two Satyre masks and cabochon sapphires.

Private collection Gianmaria Buccellati

Jeweled Medici-Style Box

1970

Lorenzo il Magnifico knew how to enjoy life and knew how necessary it was to capture fleeting time. Gianmaria Buccellati decided to concentrate magnificence in this decagonal shaped jewel box that bears the elegance of Renaissance artisanship in a harmonious combination of Florentine inspiration. The marvel of steel, gold and 266 set diamonds is worked with "modellato" engravings.

Private collection Gianmaria Buccellati

EGG OF SINS

1987

For years after he purchased it, Gianmaria Buccellati pondered on what to create with this ancient piece of malachite carved in the form of an egg.

At last he decided to display, on the egg's surface, tempting sins. The silversmiths encased the malachite with a pierced, silver-gilt mount engraving of nightmarish figures surveyed by the Devil. The inspiration for the figures came to Buccellati from the etchings of Jacques Callot (1592–1635) and in particular, from Callot's *Temptation of St. Anthony* (1634).

The techniques of piercing, engraving, modeling, chasing, and stone setting were used to decorate the antique malachite in concert with gold, silver, quartz, and lapis lazuli and malachite cabochon stones to create this impressive, albeit, peculiar object.

Private collection Gianmaria Buccellati

MEDICI-STYLE CUP

1984

The famous Medici family ruled over and directed the destiny of Florence for more than three hundred years until 1737. During their glorious rule, members of the family indulged their passion for the arts, literature and learning, helping Florence to become the greatest repository of European culture since the Athens of Pericles in the 400s BC.

Inspired by the great achievements of this Renaissance dynasty, Gianmaria Buccellati created the Medici-Style Cup, which stands as one of his finest achievements. The carved sodalite goblet is embellished with several engraved gold bands, some of which include stylized acanthus leaves while others are embellished with faceted rubies set within yellow gold rosettes.

Private collection Gianmaria Buccellati

CUPS OF MYTHOLOGY

1979

The style is inspired by the French Rococo period (1730–1770). The subject is the everlasting influence of Greek mythology on Western cultures. Gianmaria Buccellati meant to sculpt the figures inside a whirlpool of instability, represented here by fire. The object contemplates a pair of golden, covered cups, supported at the base by juxtaposed infants (putti). The cups are adorned with ivory carved medallions representing legendary mythological figures counterbalanced and surrounded by swirling shapes that recall waves of fire.

Private collection Gianmaria Buccellati

BOX OF MONTHS OF LIFE

1983

As a tribute to the passages and changes in life, Gianmaria Buccellati dedicates this unusual shaped box to life itself. Twelve inset ivory carvings and six scripted scrolls reveal the journey of life experienced by all human beings.

The upper part of the box, along with twelve cabochon emeralds set in a sphere in the midst of the leafy ivory bush, represents the spirit of longevity. The style recalls the Tudor period as much as the geometrical shapes could come from the Moresque Arabic culture. Silver and gold carvings have been created with embossing, chiseling and engraving. They are merged with the ivory, twelve cabochon sapphires and twelve cabochon emeralds, in the attempt to convey vital energy.

Private collection Gianmaria Buccellati

EVOLUTION OF MAN

1986

The style is a typical Buccellati combination of Classical inspiration with the philosophical thoughts of civilization. Beginning with ancient Greece, the journey continues through Chinese and Roman periods, crosses the Renaissance and lands on the American civilization and its frontiers of space.

Placed above the contrasting shades of color from red to green around the circular shape of the urn, is a blazing eternal flame of life. The red and green jasper squares are edged with silver linings, as well as the eight ivory carved pieces.

Private collection Gianmaria Buccellati

TRIBUTE TO WOMAN

1985

This octagonal urn was thought by Gianmaria Buccellati as a repository for the feminine spirit.

Four facets depict the main stages in the life of a woman as if they were the four seasons. The miniature plaques are carved in ivory and are set within panels of lapis lazuli and malachite. They have been executed using the graffito engraving technique, and have been set with silver and gold frames surrounding each part of the object.

Private collection Gianmaria Buccellati

LIFE IS A GAME

1984

In the sixteenth century, play acting improvised in urban piazzas was the form of protest of poor people. Many actors wore masks in order to protect themselves from being identified by the local authorities. Thus started the *Commedia dell'Arte* and the fame of masked figures like the harlequin.

Gianmaria Buccellati designed six famous masks depicting six expressions of mankind, on six facets. To seal the game of life he adds a precious carved emerald surrounded by a dense golden frame. The box, in silver and gold, is composed of six carved medallions, an emerald carved stone, and one round ivory bezel.

Private collection Gianmaria Buccellati

CRUSADES CHESS GAME

1982

Ahomage to the ancient game of chess, this version is played on a board of 32 lapis lazuli and 32 malachite squares, surrounded by a silver edge. The chessmen are inspired by the figures of Crusaders opposed to Saracens. The light figures are medieval, the dark ones are mysterious Arab-Asian warriors. The medieval figures are carved in ivory; the Saracens are in solid silver. Each piece is sculpted with an intense expression.

The game is encased in a leather box encrusted by silver rosettes topped by a carved ivory plate depicting a battle site.

Private collection Gianmaria Buccellati

Renaissance Pitcher and Basin

1987

The simple shape of this eternal container has been recreated, here, by Gianmaria Buccellati with a strong Renaissance flair.

From the tray that carries a sinuous feminine shape of an amphora, to its solid silver beak, this object has been created with perfect harmony and refined techniques.

The cabochon shaped tiles of lapis lazuli and malachite have been applied to the hand-molded silver body, overcoming a multitude of difficulties both in sculpting the stones and in setting them into the silver.

Private collection Gianmaria Buccellati

MALACHITE AND SILVER TABLE

1991

With Mario Buccellati's wit, Gianmaria designed this massive piece of Roman Baroque, a homage to Bernini, exclusively with the intent to place one exceptional piece of malachite that he possessed.

Dolphin motives were familiar sixteenth-century decorations. In a somehow surrealistic mood, the dolphins hold the malachite surface, but they seem to be fish and water, water and waves.

This masterpiece of silversmithery is 53.5 cm high and stands as a rare example of "small" furniture made as if it were a home object. The base of the table is realized with the lost wax technique and the assemblage took two years of work.

Private collection Gianmaria Buccellati

CANDELABRA

1960

The nine-branch candelabra was designed seventy years ago by Mario Buccellati who had in mind an oak tree. It was executed again by Gianmaria forty years ago.

This massive piece, realized in sterling silver, has been created with the lost wax method, and has been chiseled and fixed with invisible joints. Totally hand-made, only two of these exceptional pieces exist. It is 71 cm high and weighs nearly 20 kilograms. The diameter between the openings of the branches is 66 cm. Foliage and branches seem to dance in flames and still carry a mysterious vitality that can only come from the quality of patient silversmithery.

Private collection Gianmaria Buccellati

Boscoreale Cups

1922–24

"Silver objects are subject to the human mutability of taste. Now they want the Furnic items, then they prefer Clodio's or Grazio's. Now they want flat surfaces, then they prefer chiseled or embossed ones, or even filigree" (Plinius the Elder, 23–79 AD). Plinius died in the attempt to help the fleeing population of Pompeii during the eruption of mount Vesuvius (August 24, 79 AD). Buried by lava was a villa called "La Pisanella", near Pompeii, at Boscoreale. The site became one of the greatest finds of Roman silver in 1895: 109 objects now demonstrate the remarkable sense of style and dexterity of Roman silversmiths. Mario Buccellati's intimate knowledge of silversmithing techniques enabled him to duplicate the skills of ancient artists with exact reproductions of eight pieces of the treasure.

The most impressive elements are the relief decorations created through repeated heating and hammering from the inside. In so doing, the relief can be achieved on silver "containers" without splitting the metal. A simple gilded liner is used inside of the silver container, so as to hold food and beverages.

Private collection Gianmaria Buccellati

The Jewels of Gianmaria Buccellati

This necklace has a typical Classical design, inspired by the seventeenth century. Ten beautiful pale-blue Ceylon sapphires are set in yellow gold. This piece is a perfect example of the transition period between Mario and Gianmaria Buccellati. The necklace was created in 1975 and still belongs to a private collector in New York.

Property of a private collection in New York

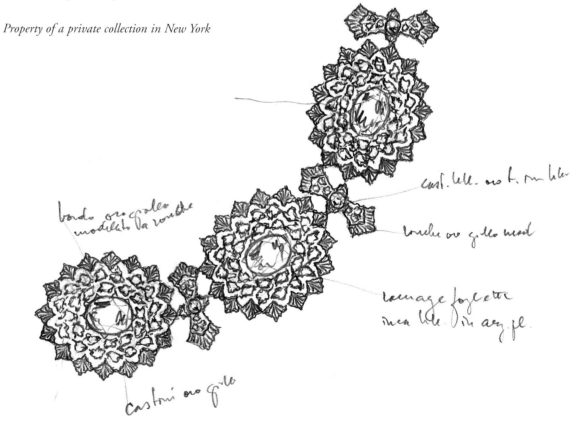

This set is also a good example of the transition period between Mario Buccellati and his son Gianmaria. The brooch was one of the first pieces Gianmaria created after his father's death. It was made for an important Milanese customer and they worked very closely on the design. The central diamond is surrounded by lace-work in yellow gold and silver.

Gianmaria designed the bracelet ten years later for the same customer, who was also a customer of his father. Again he used the sensation of lace but with a very different effect.

Property of a private collection in Milan

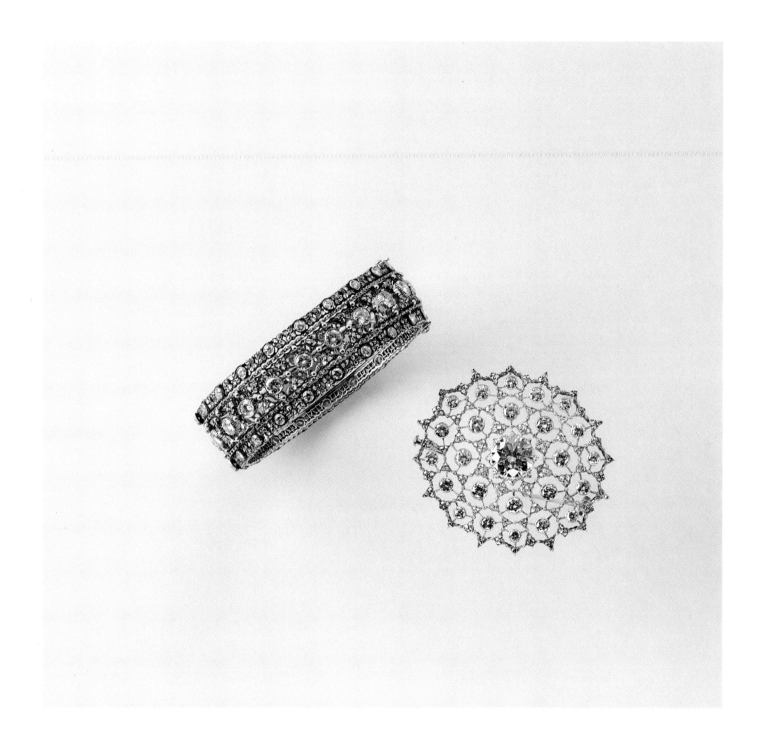

This gold trousse is one of the finest examples of the exceptional engraving that is a Buccellati hallmark. The illusion of an old damask is created by very detailed engraving on both the outside and inside. The clasp is made of diamonds, set in white gold with an important cabochon emerald in the center.

Private collection Gianmaria Buccellati

This set was created in 1985 and still belongs to its first owner. It could be called a Royal Parure for the quality of work, inspiration of design and beauty of the stones. The motif is inspired by the elegance of the bow. The white diamonds are set in white gold and the canary diamonds and emeralds in yellow gold to enhance the contrast. The yellow diamonds are distributed in a very free way all through the set.

Property of a private collection in Riyadh

The flower brooch with the end of the leaves turning up, as they do in Autumn, is a marvelously typical Buccellati theme. Gianmaria's passion and admiration for nature is often seen in his designs. As normal, this piece was created after studying a beautiful stone for a long time. The central stone is a high-quality peridot surrounded by canary diamonds set in yellow gold and white diamonds set in white gold, again, to enhance the contrast.

Property of Patricia Kennedy, Los Angeles

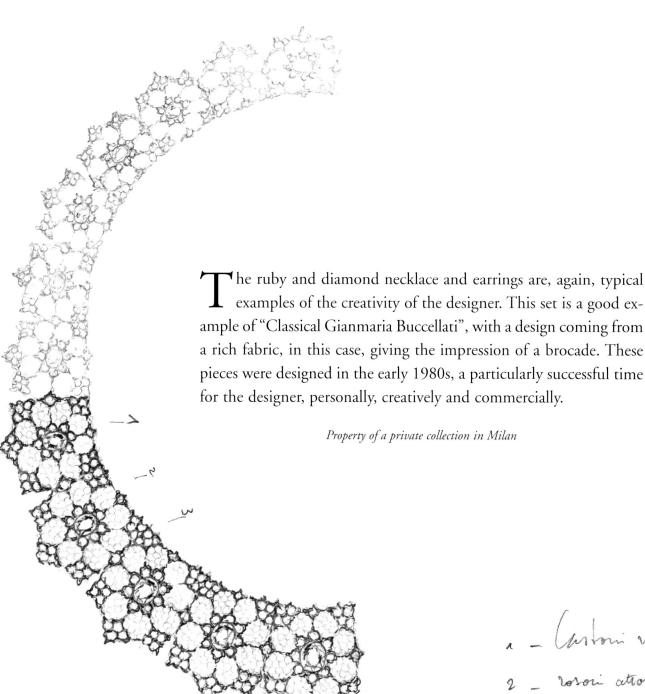

The ruby and diamond necklace and earrings are, again, typical examples of the creativity of the designer. This set is a good example of "Classical Gianmaria Buccellati", with a design coming from a rich fabric, in this case, giving the impression of a brocade. These pieces were designed in the early 1980s, a particularly successful time for the designer, personally, creatively and commercially.

Property of a private collection in Milan

1 — Castoni interni oro giallo

2 — rosoni attorno al castone e tutte le sagome esterni orob. brillete.

3 — Sagome interne a pavé in oro giallo mca brillanti.

One of the most impressive and interesting pieces from a gemology perspective, is the Phoenix brooch, named after the legend of the fabulous Phoenix bird, symbol of death, resurrection and immortality that reproduces itself from its own ashes. The body is formed by an extremely rare 136.10-carat pearl (really a concretion composed of 17 pearl nuclei) mounted in white and yellow gold. The Phoenix is decorated with 26 emeralds set in the tuft, one faceted ruby (the eye), 881 fancy natural-colored diamonds (the plumage of wings and tail and the scroll decorations underneath the body) and one light-gray baroque pearl (the ashes). This extraordinary piece, designed in 1983, vividly illustrates the wild imagination and bold creativity of Gianmaria Buccellati.

Private collection Gianmaria Buccellati

The stones were purchased in Hong Kong long before they appeared in this beautiful, delicate set of imperial jade. Gianmaria Buccellati usually acquires the stones just because he "loves" them, because he immediately feels a "special relationship", because they "sing" to him. Sometimes it takes years and many designs to come up with a good solution, and this piece is a good example of this. All the jade is irregular and to actually put all of the stones together was a difficult and very demanding adventure for some fifteen years! Finally, he found a place for all the stones, set in yellow gold. People might call him a mathematical genius, but to Gianmaria it all comes naturally.

Property of a private collection in London

To make an interesting piece of jewelry out of this extraordinary large black Australian opal, Gianmaria had to enrich the stone with a certain kind of decoration. He chose to create a net of small diamonds in a yellow-gold setting around the stone. The beautiful chain in the same pattern was added a few years later, so that this beautiful rare opal can be worn as a fascinating necklace.

Property of a private collection in New York

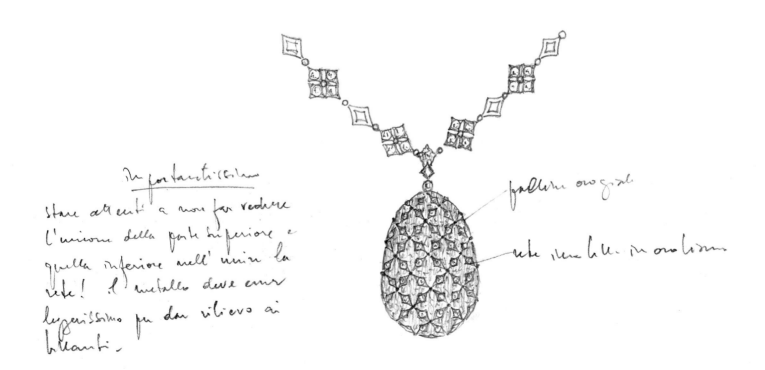

In 1988, a man came to see Gianmaria Buccellati and offered him 66 rough diamonds. At first he was not very interested since he is not a cutter and advised the man to go and see someone in Amsterdam. Not taking no for an answer, the man insisted that Mr. Buccellati have a look at them. Finally he took the diamonds out of the bag and put them in his hands, and immediately fell in love with them. It was like they were singing to him and he purchased these wonderful stones.

At first he wanted to cut them but the more he looked at his diamonds, the more he fell in love and he decided to keep them the way they were, as there was no reason to ruin their natural beauty. This important necklace with the rough diamonds surrounded by smaller cut diamonds to shape anemone flowers, is a triumph of creativity.

Property of a private collection in Stamford, CT

This bracelet was designed by Gianmaria in 1973, during the decade after his father's death and is a wonderful example of the "fusion" of Mario and Gianmaria's work. Created in perfect "Buccellati Style", this open-work bracelet features a rhombus design. It is fashioned in the typical eighteenth-century French style, "Rocaille", one of Gianmaria's favorites.

Property of a private collection in Milan

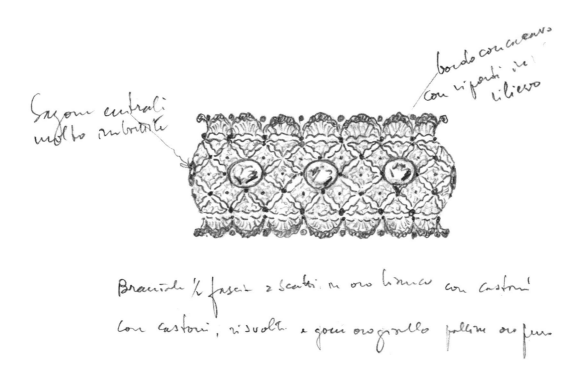

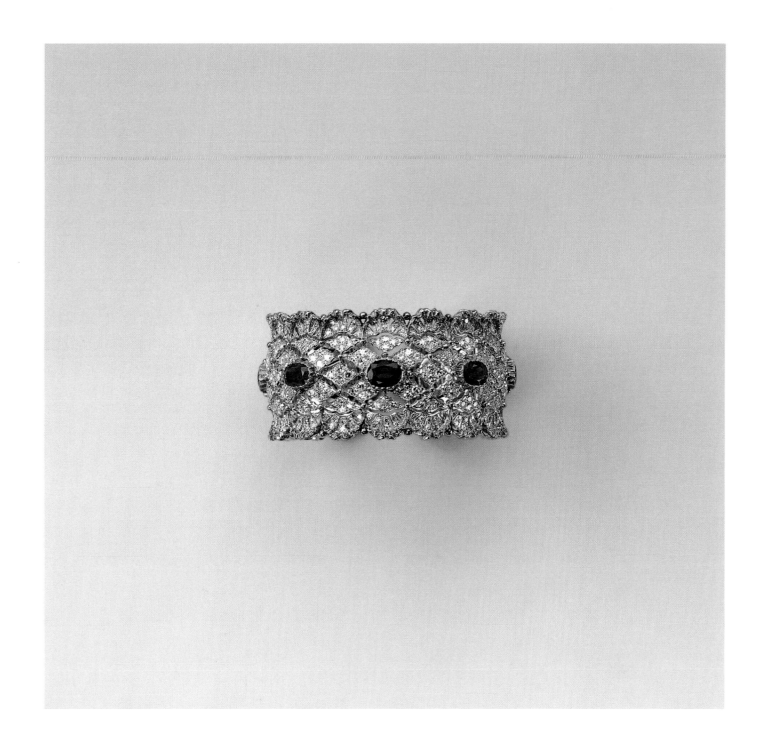

This diamond necklace with matching bracelet and earrings is fashioned after an antique piece of Venetian lace ("Pizzo Venezia") that Gianmaria saw in a lace museum in Venice. Much attention is paid to detail: for example, the border of the necklace is just like the thread in a piece of lace. Again to enhance the illusion of real lace, yellow gold is employed. The beautiful and delicate set was created in 1992.

Property of a private collection in Geneva

Created in 1966, this set is among the earliest pieces designed and executed by Gianmaria in the period following the death of his father, Mario.

Conceived in Mario's classic style, the ring and earrings feature typical lace effects and workmanship surrounding the high-quality Colombian emeralds.

Property of a private collection in New York

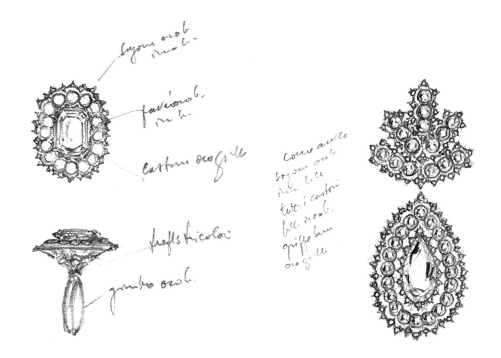

foglie monochromico
con venutvra a
taglio di sega inenble

briolette antiche da
montare con coppette
finale con perno
trasversale

The briolette diamonds used in this set were part of an ancient Indian necklace, but when Gianmaria saw them, he decided to buy it, take the stones out, and create something completely new. The end result is a beautiful Renaissance-inspired design, but seen in a more modern way.

Property of a private collection in London

The form of this spectacular Mexican opal, which was bought in 1976 in the United States, gave inspiration for many different animal designs. Finally Gianmaria choose the dragon because of its imaginative character that captivates audience. The customer prefers that it be referred to as a "griffin".

Property of a private collection in New Orleans, LA

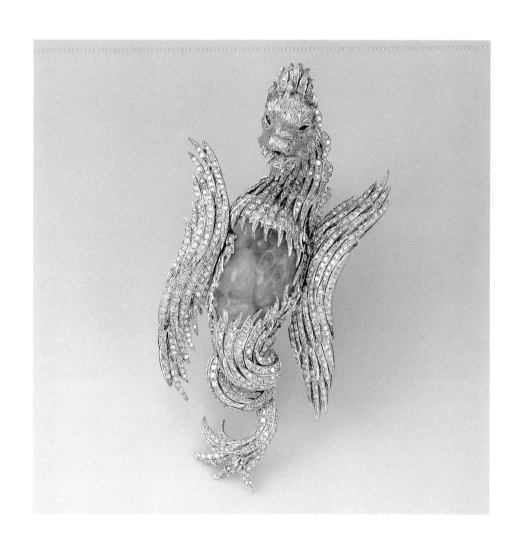

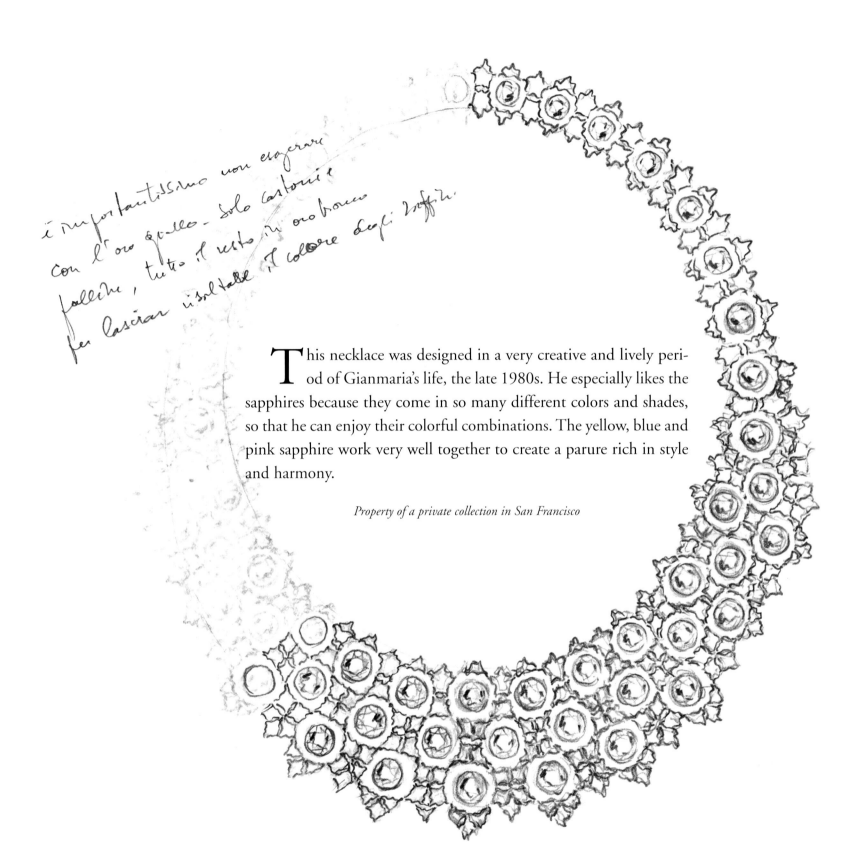

è importantissimo non esagerare con l'oro giallo - Solo castonie follicini, tutto il resto in oro bianco per lasciar risaltabe il colore degli Zaffiri.

This necklace was designed in a very creative and lively period of Gianmaria's life, the late 1980s. He especially likes the sapphires because they come in so many different colors and shades, so that he can enjoy their colorful combinations. The yellow, blue and pink sapphire work very well together to create a parure rich in style and harmony.

Property of a private collection in San Francisco

This brooch was conceived in 1972 and it is one of the few pieces Gianmaria designed directly. He saw this peacock in a Chinese painting and thought it was so poetic, beautiful and special that he wanted to make a jewel out of it.

Property of a private collection in New York

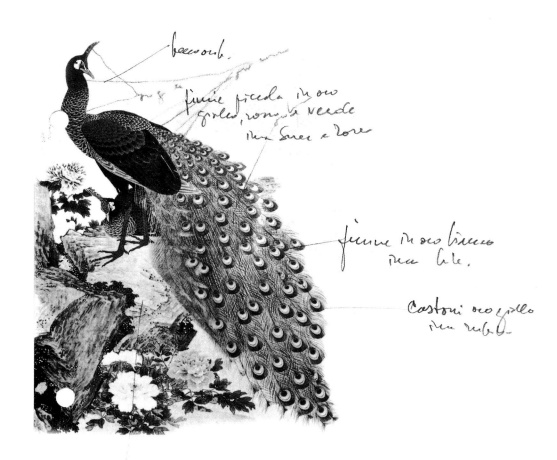

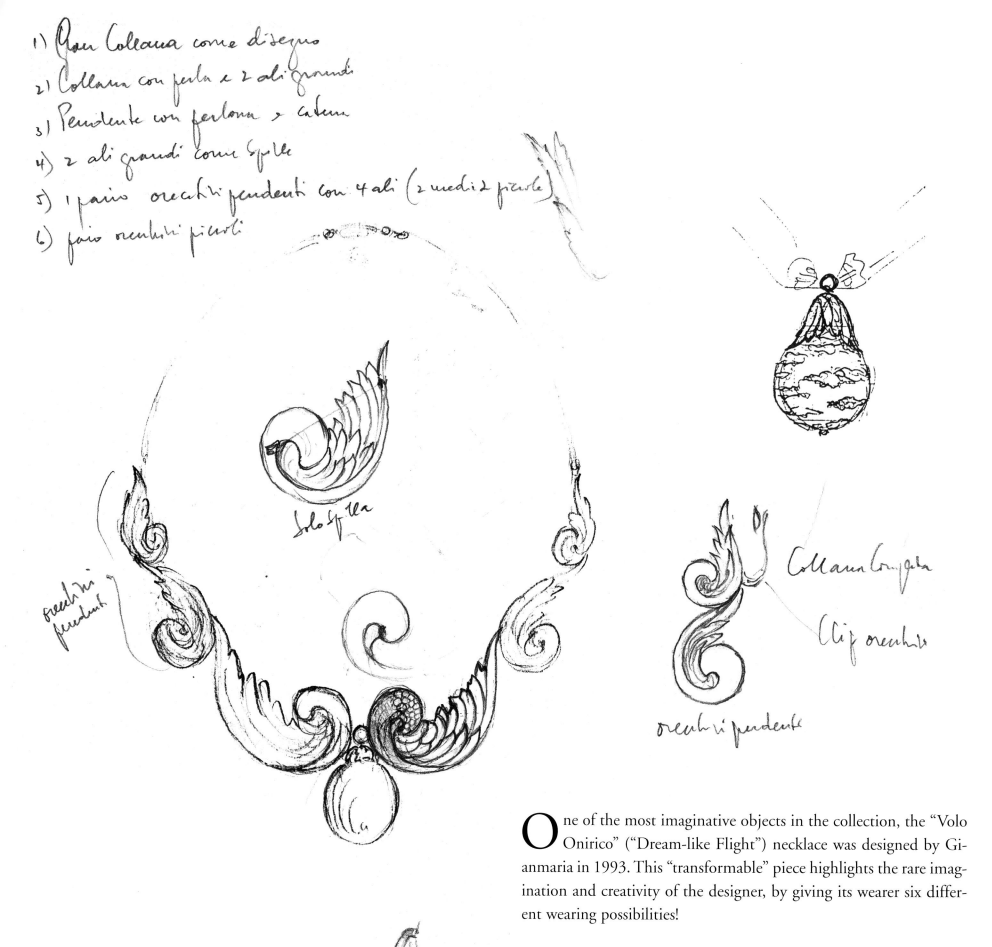

1) Gran Collana come disegno
2) Collana con perla e 2 ali grandi
3) Pendente con perlona e catena
4) 2 ali grandi come Spille
5) 1 paio orecchini pendenti con 4 ali (2 medi e piccoli)
6) paio orecchini piccoli

Solo Spilla

orecchini pendenti

Collana completa

Clip orecchini

orecchini pendente

One of the most imaginative objects in the collection, the "Volo Onirico" ("Dream-like Flight") necklace was designed by Gianmaria in 1993. This "transformable" piece highlights the rare imagination and creativity of the designer, by giving its wearer six different wearing possibilities!

Private collection Gianmaria Buccellati

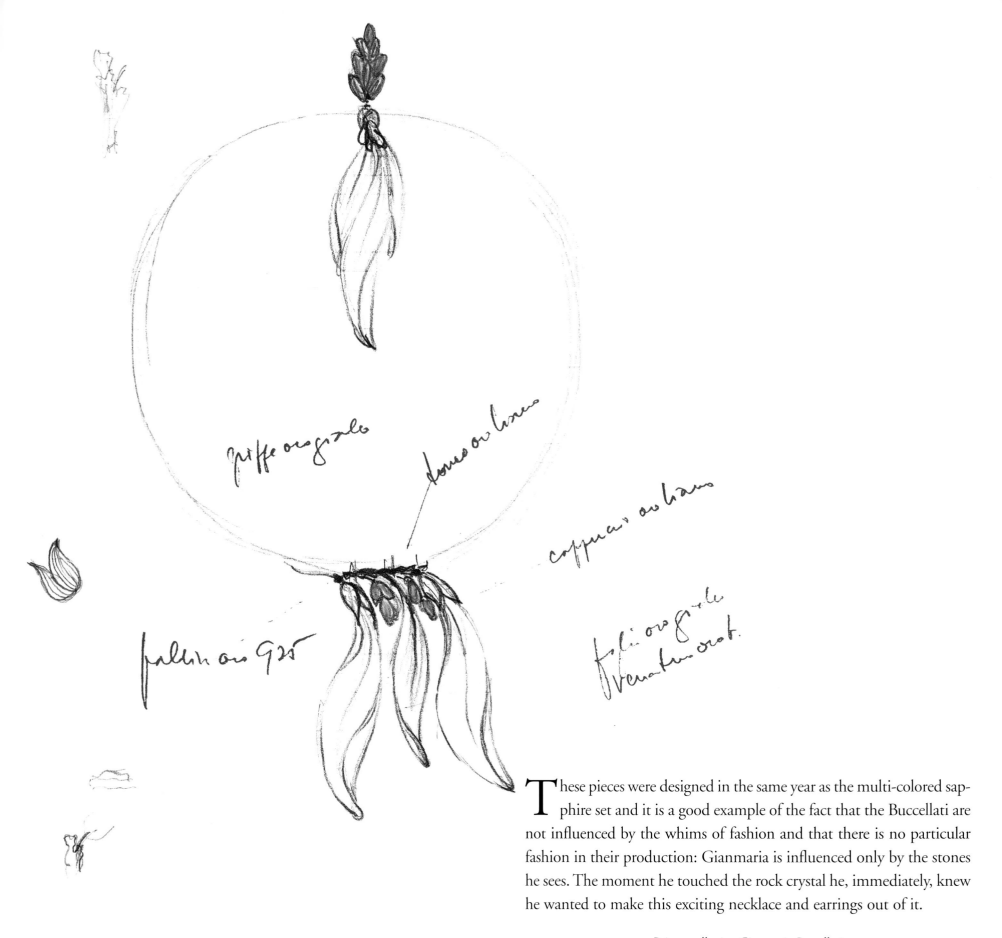

These pieces were designed in the same year as the multi-colored sapphire set and it is a good example of the fact that the Buccellati are not influenced by the whims of fashion and that there is no particular fashion in their production: Gianmaria is influenced only by the stones he sees. The moment he touched the rock crystal he, immediately, knew he wanted to make this exciting necklace and earrings out of it.

Private collection Gianmaria Buccellati

The Creation of a Honeycomb Jewel: Behind the Scene

Gianmaria Buccellati designs all of his jewels personally or with his son, Andrea. He then follows their progress through the successive stages of creation. He checks them throughout the process for perfect quality, and the fine balance between technique and aesthetic appeal. Once a piece has gone through the rigorous program, it is signed to give authenticity of its design and unique nature. The Gianmaria Buccellati signature is the "mark" that even the tiniest detail has been given attention during its creation.

The first step is the design phase and presentation to artisan: Gianmaria or Andrea prepares a detailed line sketch of the piece (in this case, a honeycomb brooch). The sketch is prepared in order to meet with the artisan so that he can present his "conception" of the jewel; to discuss the fabrication, materials, and the precise placement of the honeycomb design. The artisan enjoys a true rapport with Gianmaria, who constantly guides him through the various stages of creation.

1. Tracing

It is the goldsmith that brings the jewel to "life". He starts with a pure metal plate (here, white gold) and transforms and refines it to become a jewel. The craftsman begins by tracing the many circles or lines on the surface of the metal plate according to Gianmaria's design of the piece.

2. Piercing

Now the complicated process begins. The craftsman, using a small hand drill, pierces a hole in the middle of every circle that he traced. This process is completely manual, and requires the greatest skill and steady hand of the artisan.

3. Sawing

The artisan saws the hole with a miniature saw blade, in the shape of the honeycomb pentagon. Performing this delicate work, he has to saw with the saw blade at least five times to obtain the perfection of the honeycomb holes.

4. Polishing of the Holes

The artisan uses a very delicate thread covered with pumice paste to polish the inside surface of the honeycomb holes. This is a very time consuming and labour intensive process, as each and every hole in the piece must be methodically polished in this way.

5. Choice of Gemstones

This is an important step, as the choice of gemstones will determine the actual appearance of the jewel. They are chosen not only for color and quality, but also for the aesthetical result that is requested by the designer.

6. Gem Setting

The craftsman has the task of setting the stones called for by the design. It is demanding and difficult due to the fragility and delicate nature of the honeycomb. Each stone is "embraced" by gold as to secure the light from under it. The stone setter's work is aimed at enhancing the stones, but he must also be as delicate and skilled so as to leave the tiniest quantity of metal around the stone itself.

7. Engraving of Surface

The engraving on a honeycomb piece takes place on the very thin edges on its sides. This delicate task is necessary to provide the aesthetical results demanded of every Gianmaria Buccellati piece. The relief is created using an ancient technique, incising the surface with a graving tool called burin, which dates from the Renaissance.

8. Engraving of the Back Parts

The utmost care devoted to even the tiniest details is the hallmark of the Buccellati House. For example, the back of the jewel is often finely engraved to appear as aesthetically pleasant as the front.

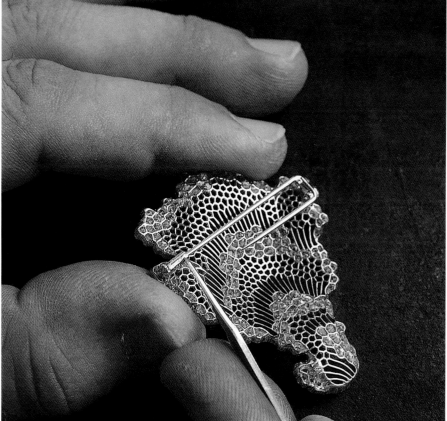

9. Painting, Cleaning and Rhodium Plating

Most Buccellati jewels are made with different colors of gold (yellow, white, or pink). Therefore, in order to obtain the final results according to the original design and to obtain the best reflection of the stones, the polisher "paints" all of the gold parts of the piece (yellow, pink, green, etc.), except for white gold, with a layer of special enamel, aimed at protecting the color surface. The piece is then washed in a chemical bath with the purpose of removing any grease and surface dirt that may have accumulated during the process of workmanship. Finally, the piece is put into a bath of Rhodium liquid where it will remain for a couple of minutes. During the Rhodium plating, the surfaces in white gold, will turn whiter and more brilliant, while, as a result of the initial painting, the protected areas will remain yellow or pink, or green. The Rhodium plating gives the jewel "dimension" and special appeal.

After the Rhodium bath, the piece will be put into a weak acid bath to remove the enamel. The jewel is then dried and cleaned and is prepared for the Quality Control Department, who will check the final details to be sure it is perfect.

It is obvious that the above described steps only tell you of the fundamental phases of the working process. As a matter of fact, in the case of items demanding months of work, there are so many more details and particulars that cannot really be described with photos or, sometimes, even with words. The jewel, having passed through many hands and checks along the way, is finished.

The various stages of work, from the original design through the final moment when the jewel is presented to the client, are carried out with meticulous care.

This is true whether the jewel is a small ring or impressive parure: all the pieces have one thing in common, that is the love and care which Gianmaria and Andrea Buccellati and their artisans lavish upon their work, both for their own pleasure, and for the pleasure of those who appreciate it.

Catalog of Objects

Dragonfly

*In silver and yellow gold, decorated by
4 nacre pearls and 9 rose-cut diamonds.
Designed by Mario Buccellati in 1931.*

Page 23

Montalbetti Cross

*Made of pierced silver and gold, the cross
is set with diamonds and rose-cut diamonds.
On its back is a hidden reliquary in finely
engraved gold.
Designed by Mario Buccellati in 1931.*

Page 27

Flexible Sapphire Bracelet

*In yellow gold and silver, embellished with
14 light-blue sapphires (38.30 cts).
Designed by Mario Buccellati in 1930.*

Page 24

Art Deco Bracelet

*In silver, yellow and white gold, decorated
with diamonds and rose-cut diamonds.
Designed by Mario Buccellati in 1925.*

Page 28

Series of Five Rings

*In yellow and white gold decorated with rose-cut
diamonds and central stones, from left to right:
emerald, ruby, sapphire, sapphire, and rose-cut
diamond.
Designed by Mario Buccellati in the 1930s.*

Page 25

Bracelets

*These two bracelets perfectly represent the tulle
or honeycomb workmanship, hallmark of the
House Buccellati. Made of silver, lined with
yellow gold, the delicacy of the open-work
is further beautified by the diamonds
set all through.
Designed by Mario Buccellati in 1925
and 1929.*

Page 29

Tiara

*Impressive and elegant tiara in white gold lined
in yellow gold, of floral and foliage design on
a delicate tulle or honeycomb workmanship base,
highlighted with diamonds and rose-cut
diamonds.
Designed by Mario Buccellati in 1929.*

Page 26

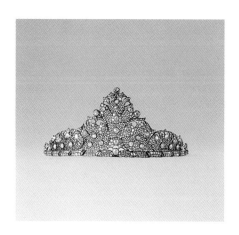

Communion Icon

*Created by Mario Buccellati for his son
Gianmaria as a souvenir of his First
Communion (April 18, 1937) and
Confirmation (May 11, 1937), at the Chapel
of the Gonzaga Institute in Milan. It is
designed as an altar, with a reproduction
of Jesus Christ and on the lateral plaques
the inscription: Gianmaria Buccellati.
Designed by Mario Buccellati in 1937.*

Page 30

Madonna Icon

Reproduction is silver of the Madonna with Saints *by Matteo di Giovanni whose original painting is shown at the Pinacoteca Nazionale in Siena.*
Designed by Mario Buccellati in 1938.

Page 31

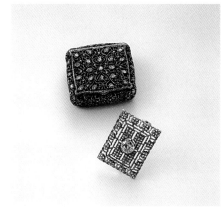

Pill Box and Rectangular Brooch

The tiny pill box is engraved in gold, with a modeled silver ramage decoration. The brooch is in silver lined in yellow gold, honey-comb worked, encrusted with diamonds.
Designed by Mario Buccellati in 1926 and 1932.

Page 35

Theater Evening Purses

These two evening purses, very popular in the 1930s, are enriched by golden clasps, decorated with diamonds and turquoises, and ruby rosettes.
Designed by Mario Buccellati in 1928 and 1929.

Page 32

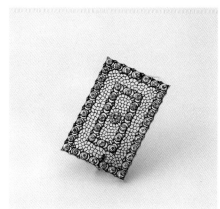

Rectangular Honeycomb Brooch

Another beautiful example of creativity. The delicate workmanship of this object focuses the importance given to details...
Designed by Mario Buccellati in 1925.

Page 35

Lapis Bracelet

Made in 925 twisted silver embellished with 5 cabochon lapis lazuli stones, this bracelet was a special order from Gabriele D'Annunzio who personally hand-signed the box.
Designed by Mario Buccellati in 1928.

Page 33

Pocket Watch with Pencil Holder

Designed by Mario Buccellati in 1933 and worn by himself until he was seventy years old.

Page 35

Necklace with Beryl Pendant

This necklace, in yellow gold decorated with 1 beryl and 87 rubies was requested to Mario Buccellati in 1923 by Gabriele D'Annunzio as he wanted to donate a "precious however peculiar" jewel to the famous actress, Eleonora Duse, to be worn as a "serto ombelicale" or belly button decoration.
Designed by Mario Buccellati in 1923.

Page 34

Sapphire Oval Brooch

Reproducing an antique lace, this brooch is made of silver lined with yellow gold, beautified with a central oval sapphire and 24 rose-cut diamonds.
Designed by Mario Buccellati in 1930.

Page 35

Jewel Box and Cigarette Cases

Executed in silver, finely chiseled, each case shows the peculiar engraving made by the House Buccellati. On the cigarette boxes are the mottos coined by D'Annunzio, often transformed by Buccellati into figuratives images. Designed by Mario Buccellati in 1934 and 1939.

Page 36

Rectangular Small Box

In yellow gold completely engraved. Designed by Mario Buccellati in 1923.

Page 37

Spectacles

Small and elegant, this object is made in white and yellow gold and is embellished with amethyst and sapphires. Designed by Mario Buccellati in1930.

Page 37

Smithsonian Cup

18K gold: 335 gr
925 silver: 278 gr
agate: 252.17 gr
40 nacre pearls: 23.69 cts
height: 14.8 cm

Page 47

Round Pill Box

Entirely made in 925 silver, it is engraved with one of the preferred mottos of Gabriele D'Annunzio, "I receive as much as I donated". Designed by Mario Buccellati in 1930.

Page 37

Cup of Pleasure

18K gold: 513.01 gr
rock crystal: 493.40 gr
faceted rubies: 9.92 cts
53 emeralds: 5.06 cts
height: 15.9 cm

Page 49

Cigarette Box

This object was made by Mario Buccellati for Gabriele D'Annunzio with the poet's own signature inside. Designed by Mario Buccellati in 1930.

Page 37

Cup of the Spirit of Love

18K gold: 1430 gr
antique red jasper: 354 gr
height: 22.8 cm

Page 51

Cup of Euphoric Bliss

18K gold: 528.8 gr
silver: 141 gr
jasper: 540.40 gr
26 faceted emeralds: 3.96 cts
2 diamonds: 0.07 cts
height: 14 cm

Page 53

Jeweled Medici-Style Box

18K gold: 1176.40 gr
steel: 111.40 gr
266 diamonds: 14.84 cts
diameter: 15.8 cm

Page 61

Cup of Muses

18K gold: 322.25 gr
925 silver: 327.58 gr
antique jade: 430.25 gr
2027 cabochon sapphires: 329.61 cts
height: 10.8 cm

Page 55

Egg of Sins

18K gold: 135 gr
925 silver: 668 gr
malachite egg: 11.223 gr
rock crystal: 2028 gr
32 cabochon lapis lazuli: 761.75 cts
12 cabochon malachites: 172.25 cts
height: 36 cm

Page 63

Rock-Crystal Candlesticks

rock crystal: 1640 gr
925 silver: 395 gr
height: 25 cm

Page 57

Medici-Style Cup

18K gold: 175.30 gr
925 silver: 274.70 gr
cup and foot in sodalite: 712 gr
64 faceted rubies: 5.76 cts
height: 21 cm

Page 65

Triumphal Amphora

18K gold: 295 gr
silver: 3250 gr
2 rock crystals: 9.201 gr
2 cabochon lapis lazuli: 149.5 cts
20 faceted sapphires: 110.17 cts
87 faceted sapphires: 22.45 cts
height: 45 cm

Page 59

Cups of Mythology

925 silver: 2053 gr
18K gold: 914 gr
ivory: 1709 gr
height: 28.5 cm

Page 67

Box of Months of Life

18K gold: 37 gr
ivory: 255.90 gr
925 silver: 2500 gr
36 cabochon sapphires: 159.26 cts
19 cabochon emeralds: 50.05 cts
diameter: 25.4 cm

Page 69

Crusades Chess Game

925 silver: 2500 gr
lapis lazuli: 1280 gr
malachite: 1120 gr
ivory : 3061.7 gr
width: 67.3 cm

Page 77

Evolution of Man

925 silver: 4040 gr
ivory: 430.95 gr
jasper: 1066.80 gr
height: 35.5 cm

Page 71

Renaissance Pitcher and Basin

925 silver: 4010 gr
37 malachites: 2590 gr
37 lapis lazuli: 1860 gr
pitcher height: 40 cm
basin diameter: 45 cm

Page 79

Tribute to Woman

18K gold: 103 gr
925 silver: 911 gr
lapis lazuli: 329.13 gr
malachite: 107.30 gr
ivory: 187.75 gr
height: 11.4 cm

Page 73

Malachite and Silver Table

925 silver: 36 kg
malachite: 33 kg
height: 53.3 cm

Page 81

Life is a Game

18K gold: 201 gr
925 silver: 2094 gr
ivory: 207 gr
1 emerald: 27.12 cts
height: 20.3 cm

Page 75

Candelabra

925 silver: 20 kg
height: 71 cm

Page 83

Boscoreale Cups

925 silver and gold plated

Page 85

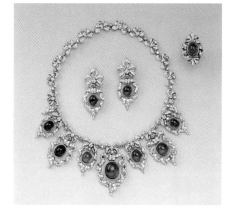

Ribbon-Design Necklace

18K white and yellow gold
7 Colombian cabochon emeralds: 72.52 cts
1173 diamonds: 259.60 cts
Matching earrings
18K white and yellow gold
2 Colombian cabochon emeralds: 15.47 cts
248 diamonds: 6.03 cts
Matching ring
18K white and yellow gold
1 Colombian cabochon emerald: 13.64 cts
220 diamonds: 3.24 cts - Page 95

Sapphire Necklace

18K white and yellow gold
10 sapphires: 89.10 cts
470 diamonds: 13.89 cts

Page 89

Sunburst Brooch

18K yellow and white gold
1 oval peridot: 29.88 cts
994 diamonds: 13.04 cts

Page 97

Pierce-work Brooch

1 central diamond: 3.40 cts
248 rose-cut diamonds: 3.00 cts
24 diamonds: 2.20 cts

Lace-work Bracelet

60 diamonds: 7.80 cts
440 rose-cut diamonds: 4.00 cts

Page 91

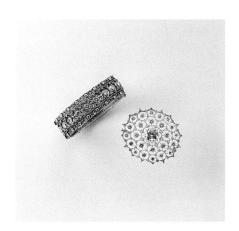

Ruby Necklace

18K yellow and white gold
20 oval rubies: 14.45 cts
1692 diamonds: 23.57 cts
Matching earrings
18K yellow and white gold
4 oval rubies: 2.45 cts
272 diamonds: 3.17 cts

Page 99

Rectangular Box

Ornato engraved in 18K yellow gold
1 cabochon emerald: 1.62 cts
180 diamonds: 3.02 cts

Page 93

Phoenix Brooch

18K white and yellow gold
1 natural born pearl conglomeration
composed of 17 nuclei: 136.10 cts
1 gray baroque pearl: 45.51 cts
26 faceted emeralds: 0.20 cts
881 natural fancy diamonds: 15.17 cts
1 ruby: 0.02 cts

Page 101

Antique Jade Necklace

18K yellow and white gold
56 jades: 31.25 cts
252 diamonds: 3.58 cts
224 rose-cut diamonds: 3.71 cts
Matching earrings
6 jades: 3.62 cts
24 diamonds: 0.44 cts
88 rose-cut diamonds: 1.29 cts
Matching bracelet
16 jades: 10.67 cts
96 diamonds: 2.07 cts - Page 103

Gold Egg Pendant

18K yellow and white gold
egg-shaped opal: 78.07 cts
161 diamonds: 1.81 cts
Matching neckchain
18K yellow and white gold
83 diamonds: 3.81 cts

Page 105

Anemone Necklace

18K yellow and white gold
53 rough-cut diamonds: 332.90 cts
661 diamonds: 11.21 cts

Page 107

Open-work Bracelet

18K pink and yellow gold
378 diamonds: 10.60 cts
5 sapphires: 5.00 cts

Page 109

Diamond Necklace

18K yellow and white gold
946 diamonds: 17.29 cts
Matching earrings
18K yellow and white gold
268 diamonds: 6.50 cts
Matching bracelet
18K yellow and white gold
448 diamonds: 6.63 cts

Page 111

Platinum Pendant Earrings

2 pear-shaped emeralds: 14.03 cts
276 diamonds: 18.80 cts
Matching ring
64 diamonds: 3.58 cts
1 emerald: 3.27 cts

Page 113

"Ramage" Necklace

18K white gold
46 briolettes: 41.01 cts
1040 diamonds: 11.01 cts
Matching earrings
10 briolettes: 2.74 cts
236 diamonds: 7.78 cts

Page 115

Griffin Brooch

18K white gold
1 Mexican opal: 42.95 cts
747 diamonds: 18.25 cts
2 marquise ruby eyes: 0.15 cts

Page 117

Fancy Sapphire Necklace

18K white and yellow gold
14 pink sapphires: 16.08 cts
21 yellow sapphires: 26.65 cts
22 blue sapphires: 29.74 cts
1090 diamonds: 10.07 cts
Matching earrings
18K white and yellow gold
6 pink sapphires: 6.87 cts
6 yellow sapphires: 6.42 cts
2 blue sapphires: 3.42 cts
96 diamonds: 2.64 cts - Page 119

Peacock Brooch

18K white and yellow gold
1 South Sea pearl: 24.15 cts
461 diamonds: 6.00 cts
163 rose-cut diamonds: 1.44 cts
74 emeralds: 1.94 cts
38 rubies: 6.49 cts

Page 121

"Volo Onirico" Necklace

18K yellow and white gold
different wearing possibilities
1 pearl: 63.45 cts
49 pearls: 198.14 cts
1 yellow diamond: 0.40 cts
439 diamonds: 9.57 cts
1133 rose-cut diamonds: 15.43 cts

Page 123

Rock-Crystal Necklace

Leaves in yellow gold
18 rock-crystal leaves: 267.60 cts
36 emeralds: 10.48 cts
36 rubies: 13.40 cts
Matching earrings
2 rock-crystal leaves: 28.16 cts
8 emeralds: 2.60 cts
8 rubies: 3.90 cts

Page 125

Acknowledgements

Buccellati Holding
Rosie Buccellati
Andrea Buccellati
Gino Buccellati
Mario Buccellati, II
Howard Hyde
Larry French
Isa Rabacchi
Sylvia Luzzatto
Shari James
All of the Loyal Artisans

**Smithsonian Institution,
National Museum of Natural History**
Robert Fri, *Director*
Robert D. Sullivan
Charles Katzenmeyer
Joseph Madeira
Heather Rostker
Kara Callaghan
Randall Kremer
Michele Urie
Ted Anderson

Italian Embassy
Ferdinando Salleo, *Ambassador*
Luigi Maccotta

*We wish to express a special thank
to all the clients who have lent their jewels
for the current exhibition*